BE A SCIENTIST!

Be a
GEOLOGIST

BY RYAN NAGELHOUT

Gareth Stevens
PUBLISHING

Please visit our website, www.garethstevens.com. For a free color catalog of all our high-quality books, call toll free 1-800-542-2595 or fax 1-877-542-2596.

Library of Congress Cataloging-in-Publication Data

Nagelhout, Ryan.
Be a geologist / by Ryan Nagelhout.
 p. cm. — (Be a scientist!)
Includes index.
ISBN 978-1-4824-1213-0 (pbk.)
ISBN 978-1-4824-1196-6 (6-pack)
ISBN 978-1-4824-1440-0 (library binding)
1. Geology — Juvenile literature. 2. Geology — Vocational guidance — Juvenile literature. I. Nagelhout, Ryan.
II. Title.
QE34.N34 2015
550—d23

First Edition

Published in 2015 by
Gareth Stevens Publishing
111 East 14th Street, Suite 349
New York, NY 10003

Copyright © 2015 Gareth Stevens Publishing

Designer: Katelyn E. Reynolds
Editor: Therese Shea

Photo credits: Cover, pp. 1, 29 Robbie Shone/Aurora/Getty Images; cover, pp. 1–32 (background texture) xpixel/Shutterstock.com; p. 4 leonello calvetti/Shutterstock.com; p. 5 Brent Lewin/Bloomberg/ Getty Images; p. 7 Henry Raeburn/Wikipedia.com; p. 8 Marco Brivio/Photographer's Choice RF/Getty Images; p. 9 Dave Souza/Wikipedia.com; p. 10 Jonathan S. Blair/National Geographic/Getty Images; p. 11 Julien Grondin/iStock/Thinkstock.com; p. 12 hsvrs/iStock/Thinkstock.com; p. 13 trotalo/iStock/ Thinkstock.com; p. 14 Yury Kosourov/Shutterstock.com; p. 15 Ralph Lee Hopkins/Lonely Planet Images/ Getty Images; p. 16 Designua/Shutterstock.com; p. 17 mehmetakgul/iStock/Thinkstock.com; p. 19 Emory Kristof/National Geographic/Getty Images; p. 20 Albert Moldvay/National Geographic/Getty Images; p. 21 Universal Images Group/Getty Images; p. 23 Gillianne Tedder/Photolibrary/Getty Images; p. 24 Dvougao/iStock Vectors/Getty Images; p. 25 David Jones/E+/Getty Images; p. 26 NASA Eugene Cernan; p. 27 NASA/JPL-Caltech; p. 28 Yarchyk/Shutterstock.com.

Printed in the United States of America

CPSIA compliance information: Batch #CS15GS: For further information contact Gareth Stevens, New York, New York at 1-800-542-2595.

CONTENTS

Words in the glossary appear in **bold** type
the first time they are used in the text.

WHAT IS A GEOLOGIST?

Geologists are scientists who study Earth. There's a lot to study! Geologists focus on Earth's rocks, **minerals**, and other matter and the processes they undergo. How the planet was formed and what makes it change are two other important topics geologists study.

In a way, geologists are Earth's historians. They learn about the history of the planet, or the events that made it the way it is today. You might wonder why that's important. Knowledge of the past helps geologists make **predictions** about the future of our world. Do you have what it takes to be a geologist? Read on to find out.

NOT JUST HARD ROCK

Geologists don't just study the rocks and minerals we see. Deep within Earth, temperatures are so hot that rocks and minerals are in a liquid state, called magma. When liquid rock comes out of Earth, it's called lava. It cools and hardens, changing Earth's surface. Magma and lava hold clues to earth-forming mysteries. However, they can be dangerous to study!

The word "geology" comes from the Latin word geologia, which means "the study of earth."

5

THE FATHER OF GEOLOGY

Though people have always been interested in how Earth works, the world's first modern geologist was James Hutton. He was born in Scotland in 1726. Though Hutton went to college to study chemistry and medicine, he became a farmer instead. Hutton became very interested in how weather changed his farmland year after year.

Many people during Hutton's time thought Earth was only about 6,000 years old. Hutton came up with a **theory** that suggested the planet was much older than that. He believed that rocks were continuously breaking down and forming new rocks, over and over again.

UNIFORMITARIANISM

Hutton's most famous theory is the Theory of Uniformitarianism. This states that Earth is being shaped by the same gradual processes today as it always has been. These changes happen at the same slow rate as well. Before Hutton's theory, scientists believed quick, powerful events such as floods formed and changed Earth.

7

Hutton gathered evidence, or proof, of his theories about Earth through observation. He observed that rocks formed in layers, with different colors and types of rock lying on top of each other. He noted how slowly these layers take shape over time. He also described how they form and break down continuously as a "great geological cycle."

Hutton thought changes on Earth were caused by heat coming from under the ground. **Volcanic eruptions** and other natural events, as well as formations like hot springs, proved this. This heat alters the world through chemical changes to rocks and the pushing and moving of Earth's outer layer, or crust.

SICCAR POINT

Hutton used rocks at Siccar Point in Scotland to support his theories. Siccar Point is a landform by the Atlantic Ocean that features two different types of rock layers slanting in different directions. Its makeup suggested to Hutton that the layers formed at different time periods in Earth's history.

These formations in Mammoth Hot Springs in Yellowstone National Park were created when water from the hot springs cooled and deposited calcium carbonate.

The different layers of rock Hutton observed are still visible today at Siccar Point.

9

IGNEOUS ROCKS

Geologists now know how rocks form. There are three main types of rocks: igneous, sedimentary, and metamorphic. Each can change into the other two forms, depending on conditions. This is the rock cycle.

VOLCANOLOGISTS

Volcanologists are geologists who study volcanoes and the processes that take place under Earth to make them erupt. They try to predict when volcanoes may erupt, which can save lives. Some volcanologists study underwater volcanoes, too! Since volcanic rock can be full of valuable minerals, some businesses are interested in hiring these geologists.

Geologists called volcanologists may wear special suits and masks to protect themselves from the gases and hot ash that erupt from volcanoes.

The speed at which magma cools often decides what kind of igneous rock is formed.

Igneous rocks are formed from magma, the hot, liquid rock deep inside Earth. Magma flows up through cracks in the ground. It may get trapped in hollow pockets where it cools to become "intrusive" igneous rock. Geologists discovered that slow-cooling underground igneous rocks have big crystals, like those found in granite.

If the magma reaches the surface, such as lava erupting from a volcano, it cools quickly to form "extrusive" igneous rock. Fast-cooling lava produces rock such as pumice, which is light and full of holes.

SEDIMENTARY ROCKS

Igneous rocks can form quickly once a volcano erupts, but the other two types of rocks form more slowly. Sedimentary rocks are made of bits of rock, sand, shells, and other matter that have been worn down by weathering. Weathering is a process in which water, ice, snow, and wind break down rocks into smaller pieces. These bits may be carried by wind, water, or ice to another place, where they settle. This is the process of **erosion**.

Sediment, which is what the bits are called, collects and hardens into rock as a layer. Layers press down on other layers over time. They're easy to spot in exposed rock formations such as cliffs.

ROCKS WEATHERING ROCKS

When wind picks up sand, it can travel great distances. Geologists discovered that the Grand Canyon was formed after millions of years of weathering not only by water, but also by blowing sand. Layers of sand sediment, called sandstone, are still visible. By knowing how the rock cycle works, geologists have explained how many amazing landforms were created.

Fossils are only found in sedimentary rocks.

The Grand Canyon's sedimentary rock layers range in age from 200 million to 2 billion years old!

13

METAMORPHIC ROCKS

The word "metamorphism" is from Greek words meaning "change of form." Metamorphic rocks were once sedimentary or igneous rocks but changed form because of heat and pressure deep inside Earth. Extreme conditions result in rocks changing **texture**, appearance, and even chemical makeup.

gneiss

Metamorphic rocks often have ribbons or waves of minerals in different colors because of different levels of heat and pressure applied to the rock over time. They may have shiny crystals in them, too. A movement of Earth's crust called uplift, as well as weathering and erosion, brings metamorphic rocks to the surface.

TYPES OF ROCKS

TYPE OF ROCK	HOW IT'S FORMED	FEATURES	EXAMPLES
igneous	cooling magma and lava	crystals, glassy, holes from gas bubbles	basalt, obsidian, pumice
sedimentary	bits of rocks, minerals, and other materials pressed together	layers may include fossils, breaks easily	coal, limestone, sandstone
metamorphic	heat and pressure within Earth	mineral "ribbons" and layers, crystals	gneiss, marble, slate

Studying metamorphic rocks helps geologists understand the effects of heat and pressure on rocks and minerals.

15

OUR PUZZLING EARTH

Besides uncovering the rock cycle, geologists have worked for centuries to unlock many of Earth's mysteries. They've discovered that Earth's outer layer works like a puzzle. It's made up of broken pieces, or plates, that slowly move. There are dozens of plates, and the major continents rest on the biggest plates.

The theory of Earth's outer layer consisting of many moving pieces is called plate tectonics.

Juan de fuca plate

North American plate

Eurasian plate

Arabian plate

Filipino plate

Caribbean plate

African plate

Cocos plate

Pacific plate

Indian plate

Pa

South American plate

Nazca plate

Easter plate

Australian plate

Juan Fernandez plate

Scotia plate

Antarctic plate

From a point above Earth, it's easy to see where two plates may be interacting to create landforms.

These "tectonic" plates move many different ways. They can grind past each other and cause **earthquakes**. Some push together to create mountains. They can move continents closer together or farther apart. By studying movements in the past, geologists can predict where the continents will move in the future.

SEISMOLOGY AND PALEOSEISMOLOGY

Some geologists focus on earthquakes. They're called seismologists. Paleoseismology is the study of **prehistoric** earthquakes. Paleoseismologists study the timing, location, and size of these earthquakes. They look for prehistoric faults, or breaks in Earth's crust. These may hold prehistoric rock and soil that can tell us what Earth was like thousands of years ago.

17

ONE CAREER, MANY CHOICES

People interested in a career in geology need to be ready to study. At the very least, geologists attend college for 4 years. They major in geology but also study math, history, and many kinds of science. After they graduate, they may work for private businesses such as mining or energy companies. They may work for the government, too.

Many geologists choose to stay in school and earn a master's or doctoral degree. Then, they can become teachers or do important **research**. They can also specialize in their studies to become paleoseismologists, volcanologists, **mineralogists**, or another kind of geologist.

START WITH SOIL

Even the dirt in your backyard is interesting to a geologist. Soil is made up of rocks and minerals ground into powder. There are also living and dead things in there! All these offer plants a healthy place to grow. Because of geologists, we know it takes millions of years to make soil.

Many geologists do fieldwork at least part of the time. The rest of their time is spent in science labs, classrooms, or offices preparing reports and using computers.

19

STUDYING OUTSIDE

Many geologists choose to teach at colleges and universities. Part of the time, they instruct students in the classroom. However, they also take classes into the field to study different kinds of land formations, show proof of Earth's processes, and observe changing surroundings to learn about an area's geologic history. Sometimes, this means traveling to locations around the globe!

Some schools ask geology teachers and students to research and publish their findings. There are many colleges all over the country that offer geology programs. If you're interested in geology, you should see if one of these schools is near you.

GLACIOLOGISTS

Another form of geology doesn't focus on rocks at all. Glacial geologists, or glaciologists, study ice, including snow, sea ice, glaciers, and ice sheets. They examine how snow and ice affect Earth today as well as how they affected it in the past. Glaciologists often work in places like Antarctica, Greenland, and the Arctic.

A geology class examines rock formations in England.

21

WORKING IN MINING

Geologists who work for mining companies locate valuable minerals, called ores, in the ground and figure out the best way to remove them. Ores may be valuable themselves or valuable for what they contain, such as the elements copper, silver, or gold. It can be costly to dig for ore, so a geologist figures out the best areas to mine. Geologists also help make maps for constructing tunnels and plan methods for workers to remove ores.

Rare earth elements are important today to mining companies and the geologists they employ. Much of the **technology** we use, such as televisions, cell phones, and computers, contains rare earth elements.

RARE OR NOT?

Rare earth elements, such as cerium and scandium, aren't actually rare. They're found all over the world, but they don't often collect in large amounts in one place. This makes geologists essential to mining companies. Without a geologist, companies wouldn't know where or how deep to dig, or when to stop looking!

A mine geologist needs many business skills as well as knowledge of Earth and its materials.

23

WORKING WITH ENERGY

Energy companies need geologists to locate fuel sources such as natural gas, coal, and oil. These form over millions of years as a result of great pressure on plant and animal remains buried deep within Earth. That's why they're called fossil fuels. The kind of fuel produced is decided by where the matter is forming underground, the temperature there, and the matter surrounding it.

Geologists can find new sources of oil and gas by collecting and **analyzing** samples of rock and soil. If they're like samples found near known **deposits** of oil and gas, there may be a supply nearby. Geologists even analyze samples from the ocean floor!

FRACKING

One way companies get natural gas is through a process called **hydraulic** fracturing, or fracking. This involves drilling into the ground and pumping in water mixed with chemicals to break up, or fracture, rocks. Natural gas then bubbles to the surface. Geologists also study the impact fracking can have on an area's land and water.

oil drilling platform

Geologists often find fossil fuels by searching for sedimentary layers that trap them.

25

GEOLOGIST IN SPACE!

Geologists study Earth and all the materials and processes it contains. However, they can use this knowledge to learn about other planets and space objects, too. Geologists who work for NASA (National Aeronautics and Space Administration) study moons, planets, and other space objects. After all, these are made of the same matter as Earth.

HARRISON SCHMITT

Harrison Schmitt was the twelfth and last person to walk on the moon. He's also the only geologist to visit the moon! Schmitt worked for NASA and went to the moon with the Apollo 17 space mission, landing on December 11, 1972. He later served as a US senator.

Harrison Schmitt spent 22 hours and 4 minutes on the moon's surface.

The Curiosity rover landed on Mars in 2012. It has many tools to help NASA geologists and other scientists explore Mars.

Scientists are finding out a lot about Mars with the help of a machine called a rover. It travels on the planet's surface, takes photos, and collects rock samples. It can actually analyze the rocks, too. Geologists now believe that Mars has plate tectonics, just like Earth!

YOU CAN BE A GEOLOGIST

Being a geologist means you're never far from your work. The entire Earth is your science lab, and there's always something new to discover. But being a geologist is much more than the ground beneath you. Your studies can take you all over the world—or into outer space!

You don't have to wait until you're in college to learn about geology. Find out what rocks and minerals make up your city and town. You can go to a local park or visit a museum. There may even be a geology or rock-collecting club at your school. If there isn't, start one!

WORKING TOGETHER

A geologist's work may lead them to work with other scientists. Engineering geologists help decide where to construct dams, pipelines, and roads. If they find strange minerals as they dig, they may call in a mineralogist to find out what they are. Sharing discoveries helps us all figure out more about our world.

GLOSSARY

analyze: to find out what something is made of

deposit: an amount of a mineral in the ground that built up over a period of time

earthquake: a shaking of the ground caused by the movement of Earth's crust

erosion: the transporting of weathered matter by water, wind, or ice

hydraulic: operated using the pressure of a liquid

mineral: matter in the ground that forms rocks

mineralogist: one who studies minerals and their features

prediction: the act of guessing what will happen in the future based on facts or knowledge

prehistoric: having to do with the time before written history

research: studying to find something new

technology: the way people do something using tools and the tools that they use

texture: the structure, form, and feel of something

theory: a general idea that explains something

volcanic eruption: the bursting forth of hot, liquid rock from within the earth

FOR MORE INFORMATION

BOOKS

Gosman, Gillian. *What Do You Know About Rocks?* New York, NY: PowerKids Press, 2013.

Hopping, Lorraine Jean. *Space Rocks: The Story of Planetary Geologist Adriana Ocampo.* New York, NY: Franklin Watts, 2005.

Mullins, Matt. *Geoscientist.* Ann Arbor, MI: Cherry Lake Publishing, 2013.

WEBSITES

Geology for Kids
kidsgeo.com/geology-for-kids/
Explore this online geology textbook for kids.

The Rock Cycle Diagram
learner.org/interactives/rockcycle/diagram.html
Click on the pictures of this interactive rock cycle.

Schoolyard Geology
education.usgs.gov/lessons/schoolyard/index.html
Find fun activities to turn your schoolyard into a geological dig.

INDEX